NATIONAL
GEOGRAPHIC

HOPING FOR RAIN

The Dust Bowl Adventures of
Patty and Earl Buckler

KATE CONNELL

PICTURE CREDITS
Cover, p. 40 Western History Collection, University of Oklahoma
Library; pp. 1, 6 (top right, middle left, middle, and right, bottom
middle), 8–9, 10, 16–17, 19 (bottom), 20 (top and bottom), 26, 30
(top), 32, 34, 36–37 Courtesy of the Library of Congress; pp. 2–3,
14–15 Courtesy Rochelle Lacy; pp. 4–5 Archives and Manuscript
Division of the Oklahoma Historical Society; pp. (bottom right), 6–7,
7 (top), 13, 18–19 Courtesy of the National Archives; p. 6 (bottom
left) John Collier/USDA Historical Photograph Collection; p. 6 (frame)
courtesy Steven Curtis Design; pp. 6 (top left), 35, 39 Hulton|Archive/
Getty Images; pp. 8 (top), 19 (top), 27 (right), 30–31 Curt Teich
Postcard Archive; pp. 8, 19, 27 (postcard) Steven Curtis Design; pp.
10–11 Picture Perfect Images; p. 12 Kansas State Historical Society;
p. 21 (top) CPIO Classic Radios; p. 21 (bottom) National Geographic
Image Collection; pp. 22–23, 24–25, 28–29 CORBIS; p.27 (left)
Phillips Petroleum Co., pp. 37 (top), 38 Los Angeles Public Library.

Connell, Kate.
  Hoping for rain : the Dust Bowl adventures of Patty and Earl Buckler
/ by Kate Connell.
  ISBN: 0-7922-6903-9 p. cm. — (I am American)
  Summary: Illustrated text, letters, and diary excerpts follow the
fictional Buckler family during the Great Depression, as they leave
Oklahoma, because of drought and duststorms, and move to
California to find work and a better life.
  1. Great Plains—History—20th century—Juvenile literature.
2. Depressions—1929—Great Plains—Juvenile literature. 3.
Dust storms—Great Plains—History—20th century—Juvenile
literature. 4. Droughts—Great Plains—History—20th century—
Juvenile literature. 5. Farm life—Great Plains—History—20th
century—Juvenile literature. 6. Farmers—Great Plains—Social
conditions—20th century—Juvenile literature. 7. Great Plains—
Social conditions—20th century—Juvenile literature. [1. Great
Plains—History. 2. Depressions—1929. 3. Dust storms—Great
Plains. 4. Droughts—Great Plains. 5. Farm life—Great Plains.]
I. Title. II. Series.
  F595.C76 2004
  978'.09'04—dc22
                          2003019126

Produced through the worldwide resources of the National
Geographic Society, John M. Fahey, Jr., President and Chief
Executive Officer; Gilbert M. Grosvenor, Chairman of the Board; Nina
D. Hoffman, Executive Vice President and President, Books and
Education Publishing; Ericka Markman, President, Children's Books
and Education Publishing Group; Nancy Feresten, Vice President,
Children's Books, Editor-in-Chief; Steve Mico, Vice President
Education Publishing Group, Editorial Director; Marianne Hiland,
Editorial Manager; Anita Schwartz, Project Editor; Tara Peterson,
Editorial Assistant; Jim Hiscott, Design Manager; Linda McKnight,
Art Director; Diana Bourdrez, Anne Whittle, Photo Research; Matt
Wascavage, Manager of Publishing Services; Sean Philpotts,
Production Coordinator; Jane Ponton, Production Artist; Susan
Donnelly, Children's Books Project Editor. Production: Clifton M.
Brown III, Manufacturing and Quality Control.

PROGRAM DEVELOPMENT
Gare Thompson Associates, Inc.

BOOK DESIGN
Steven Curtis Design, Inc.

CONSULTANTS/REVIEWERS
Dr. Margit E. McGuire, School of Education, Seattle University,
Seattle, Washington.

NATIONAL GEOGRAPHIC SOCIETY
1145 17th Street N.W.
Washington, D.C. 20036-4688

ISBN: 978-0-7922-6903-8

Printed in Spain
15/CII/2

Table of Contents

The Dirty Thirties

The Great Depression of the 1930s was a hard time for our country. Millions of Americans were out of work. Banks closed. Factories shut down. Businesses failed. Many people became poor and homeless.

In the southern Great Plains, the situation was especially bad. A severe **drought,** or long period of low rainfall, began in the early 1930s. It dried out the soil. Then, strong winds blew the dry soil into the air, creating huge dust storms. These "black blizzards" killed crops and covered everything with dirt. They blew so often that the region became known as the **Dust Bowl.**

Farmers in the Dust Bowl struggled to survive. Among them was the Buckler family of Oklahoma. Although the Bucklers are fictional, they are like most Great Plains farmers in the 1930s. Farmers depended on rainfall to grow their crops. They got drinking water from a deep well. Now, with drought, dust storms, and the Depression, they faced hard times as never before. This is the story of how they survived the "Dirty Thirties."

Area with severest damage
Dust Bowl area

"If you would like to have your heart broken, just come out here. This is the dust-storm country. It is the saddest land I have ever seen." —reporter Ernie Pyle, Garden City, Kansas, 1936

MEET THE BUCKLER FAMILY

Grandma Buckler

Grandpa Buckler

Jack Buckler, uncle

Ruth "Ma" Buckler,
mother

Wally "Pa" Buckler,
father

Pete, 8

Patty, 12

Earl, 16

CHAPTER 1

Black Sunday

As the year 1935 began, farmers in the Dust Bowl hoped and prayed for rain. Without rain, there would be no wheat crop. Without wheat to sell, there would be no money to pay bills. If the bills didn't get paid, a farm family could lose their farm.

The Bucklers were better off than some people were. They owned their 320-acre farm. They did not owe money to the bank. But they knew others who had lost their farms and moved away. Some headed west to try their luck in California. Everyone believed there was plenty of farm work in California.

The Bucklers' son Earl had left too. He had stayed home into the fall to help plant the winter wheat. Then, promising his mother that he would write, he'd said good-bye. He hitchhiked to the nearby town of Guymon and hopped a freight train heading west. Riding the rails, he soon reached Los Angeles.

January 19, 1935

Dear Ma, Pa, and all,

Hello from California! Hope you're fine. I'm picking oranges near Los Angeles. I've met lots of fellows from Oklahoma. Are you getting any rain yet? Happy birthday to Patty. Look for a package from me.

Love, Earl

P.S. I saw the Pacific Ocean!

Postcard from California

from Patty's diary

February 21, 1935

This little book is my birthday present from Earl in California. He sent it in a box with six oranges and six lemons. The oranges were so sweet and juicy! I wish they weren't all gone.

School let out early today because a big duster blew in. We had to light the lamps around noon, it was so dark. The mailman didn't come. We had lemon pie at supper, but it was dirty on top. Ma was mad she had to scrape the meringue off. Now we're trying to listen to the radio. It's mostly static because of the storm. Grandpa is letting Pete win at checkers. Ma and Grandma are sewing. Soon, we'll shake out the sheets and go to bed.

Good night, little diary.

Dear Earl,   March 10, 1935

    I am sending this to the company address you
gave me. I hope it reaches you before you move on.
    We enjoyed the fruit you sent very much. Patty
writes most every night in her diary.
    We are right in the thick of the black
blizzards. Seems the dust never stops blowing.
And how it piles up! Your friends, the Vernons,
their attic floor caved in from the dust.
    The wheat finally sprouted after some snow in
December, but it's mostly withered now. We badly
need rain. There'll be a prayer meeting for rain
next Sunday in Guymon.
    I've made a few dollars selling eggs and chickens.
The government relief money helps too. Your Pa
tore the old Model T truck down and is working
on it. Maybe he'll get it running again.
    I'll close now. We all send our love,
                                          Ma

from Patty's diary
April 14, 1935

Oh my, what a day! The darkest day yet! Diary, I think the world might be ending.

The day started clear. The sky was pure blue. We all wanted to be outside, so Ma, Grandma, and I did a big wash. Uncle Jack started on the hen-house roof, and Pa worked on the truck. Grandpa took Pete into town.

All of a sudden, it got real cold. The birds started acting strange. They flew into the yard, lots of them. Then we saw it, a huge black cloud on the horizon. It was coming from the north. Ma yelled to get in the house. We grabbed our laundry and ran.

We got in and shut up the house as best we could. Ma stuffed an old dishtowel under the door. Now we are sitting in the dusty gloom. The lamp is lit. There is dirt everywhere—in my eyes, my hair, my mouth. Ma stays at the window, looking for the car. It is darker than midnight. All we can do is wait.

A Dust Cl
Stovall

April 21, 1935

Dear Earl,

We have just passed through the worst black blizzard yet. It rolled in last Sunday. It's a mercy we are all alive.

Grandpa and Pete were driving back from Guymon when it hit. Grandpa pulled over because he couldn't see. He said it was like driving into a solid wall of dirt. Then the car died. Thank heaven they didn't try to walk home. But they were nearly buried sitting in the car. After the wind died down some, Pa took the tractor and brought them home.

Pa and Uncle Jack got the animals into the barn, then couldn't see to get to the house. One calf had wandered off and was suffocated. I'm sorry to lose it. The mother is restless and unhappy. I can imagine how she feels. We came close to a tragedy last Sunday.

Now Pete and Grandpa are both coughing their lungs to pieces. Otherwise, we are holding up okay.

With love from,
Ma and the family

ay April 14, 1935
d Rolling Over The Pra
dio Dodge City, Kansas #3

People who were caught in dust storms, like Grandpa Buckler and Pete, often got sick. A new type of lung illness soon became common in the Dust Bowl. It was called dust pneumonia. People with dust pneumonia coughed a lot and had trouble breathing. Some people died from it.

In the spring of 1935, the Red Cross set up six emergency hospitals in the Dust Bowl states. Red Cross volunteers handed out 17,000 gauze masks. Red Cross doctors and nurses visited hundreds of homes to help people who were sick from the dust.

In Guymon, two church basements were turned into emergency hospitals. Wally drove Grandpa and Pete to one of those hospitals. Both had been coughing up dirt. They were given medicine and put in **oxygen tents** to help them breathe. After a few days, they were sent home with dust masks. They were given instructions on how to "dust proof" their house. Unfortunately, there was little else doctors could do.

Red Cross volunteers wear dust masks.

CHAPTER 2

Dust, Dust Everywhere

The spring dust storms of 1935 drove many people out of the southern Great Plains. In one month, 100 families left Texas County, Oklahoma, where the Bucklers lived.

Yet, the Bucklers were determined to stay. They had farmed their land since 1906. That was the year Grandma and Grandpa came to Oklahoma Territory as **homesteaders.** Wally and Jack were just little boys then. They had gone through some rough times growing up. They believed they would get through this time too.

The Bucklers set about dust proofing their home as well as they could. They stuffed rags around the window and doorframes. They covered the windows with old sheets. On dirty days, Grandma waved a wet dishtowel through the air to collect dust. At night, they slept with wet cloths over their faces.

The dust got in anyway, no matter what they did to stop it. Dust became part of the Bucklers' lives. They wore it on their clothes, ate it in their food, and combed it out of their hair. They cursed it. They joked about it. And they prayed for it to end.

The screen over this window can't keep the dust away from this boy and his family.

from Patty's diary

May 1, 1935

Did you hear the one about the farmer who fainted when a raindrop hit him on the head? They had to throw three buckets of sand in his face to wake him up.

Starting today, I'm writing down jokes to tell Earl when he comes home. Here's one Pete heard: Did you see the flock of birds flying backwards? That's how they keep the sand out of their eyes.

June 6, 1935

This morning I found a baby jackrabbit in the kindling pile. He was shaking and didn't fight me when I picked him up. One of his eyes was blinded by dust. I washed his eye and put him in a box to rest. I hope this one lives. The jackrabbits we found in the yard after Black Sunday both died.

June 7, 1935

I am so sick and tired of boiled wheat cereal for breakfast! I can tell only you, Diary. Ma would scold if I complained. Lots of folks haven't got as much as we have. I do wish Earl would send more oranges!

Uncle Jack said to name my jackrabbit FDR. He says it stands for Finest Darn Rabbit.

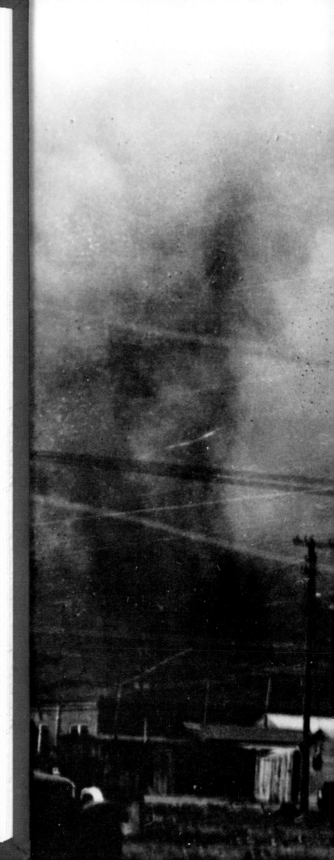

Dear Earl,   June 8, 1935

Just a line to say we are holding up. We had some cleanup after Black Sunday! I carted bushels of dirt out of the house. There were a few broken windows and such like. All my clean laundry got dirty, so I had to wash it again. My curtains are ruined, but I can't replace them, so there they hang.

We have had a couple of light rains. Folks are hoping the drought is breaking. It won't save the wheat, though. We went ahead and planted some feed crops. There's no grass for the cattle. They're eating weeds. The Vernons are shipping their stock east to pasture. Pa thinks it's too expensive. It's hard, but we'll get by. We've still got enough from the big harvest in '31.

Are you thinking of coming home? Pete's writing a little song for you on Grandpa's old guitar.

Love from us all,
Ma

June 30, 1935

Dear Earl,
   I hope this reaches you. We are wondering why we haven't heard back from you. Are you thinking of staying out there forever?
   We've had two rains this month, and it's been real hot. Hardly a day passes without dust blowing over. Grandma makes Grandpa wear a dust mask when he's outdoors. She gets mad if he won't. I wish Pa and Jack would wear masks, but they are too stubborn. I do my outdoor work in a big shade hat with a handkerchief tied over my face. I believe I scared the chickens!
   Folks are saying that the government's going to take the land away and make us all move. Well, we won't go. We're not quitters. Anyway, I don't believe President Roosevelt would do that to us. But the rumors are flying, along with the everlasting dust.
   It's nearly noon and I hear the cows mooing. I suppose they want water, so I'll close.

                                    With love from all,
                                    Ma

from Patty's diary
July 16, 1935

Dear Diary — We drove into town last Sunday for a prayer service for rain. As soon as we got home, a terrific duster blew in. I guess we didn't pray hard enough. Today I cleaned the animals' nostrils twice and the leaves of the geraniums in the kitchen once. Now I have to sweep. There are ripples of dust on the kitchen floor.

P.S. FDR is feeling much better. Pa says to let him go, but I don't want to. I put him in the old rabbit hutch.

July 25, 1935

Joke for Earl: A man was driving down the road and saw a ten-gallon hat sitting on a dust drift. He looked under it and saw a man's head. "Need any help?" he asked the head. "Need a ride into town?" "Much obliged," said the head. "But I'll get there on my own. I'm on a horse."

August 21, 1935

Dear Earl,

We've been real busy. Pa's been plowing the fields. That's to keep rain from running off, if we get any. There's been no rain since early July. Pa is using a machine on loan from the county. The Vernons will use it after us.

Today I swept (twice), dusted, churned butter, watered the hens, and mended Pete's pants. After lunch, Grandma, Patty, and I listened to a play on the radio and looked at the new Sears catalog. There's one or two dresses I might get Patty for school with my egg money. I've let her hems down as far as they can go.

Last Sunday, we drove out early to see the dinosaur pit in the next county. The state university is digging up the old bones. We saw them working on a thighbone four feet long! We had a picnic and got back by nightfall. Uncle Jack stayed behind to look after the animals. It was hot, but it didn't blow, and we had a nice time.

On the road, we saw hardly any cars but quite a few abandoned farms. A lot of folks have left.

We miss you. I often hear Patty and Pete wishing for their brother to come home. I feel the same.

Love from all,
Ma

P.S. Pa got the old Ford truck running!

September 1, 1935
Dear folks,
   I'm in the San Joaquin Valley trying to get work as a picker. I'm fixing to head home soon. It's pretty rough here, but I'll tell you about it when I see you.

Love to all,
Earl

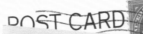

POST CARD

GREETINGS from CALIFORNIA

523

© C. T. & CO.

8A-H536

Dorothea Lange, famous photographer

from Patty's diary
September 6, 1935
Guess what? Uncle Jack met a lady photographer working for the government. She stopped her car and asked if she could take a picture of Grandpa on the tractor in his dust mask. At supper, when Grandma declared it was a waste of government money, Jack said photographers have to eat too. Ma said, "Especially lady photographers, right, Jack?" He just raised his eyebrows like he does.

During the 1930s, the federal government created programs to help people who were struggling because of the Depression. President Franklin Delano Roosevelt (known as FDR) called the programs the **New Deal**. The New Deal created jobs for all sorts of workers, from photographers to farmers.

The presence of government agents in Great Plains states led to rumors that people would be forced off their land. But Dust Bowl farmers actually got help from a New Deal agency called the Soil Conservation Service, or SCS. People at the SCS believed that new farming methods would stop soil **erosion** and cut down on the dust.

The southern Great Plains had once been covered with grasses. The grasses needed little rain. Their deep roots held the soil, even when strong winds blew. Then, in the 1910s and 1920s, millions of acres were plowed up and planted with wheat. When the drought began in 1931, the wheat died. Soon there was nothing to hold the soil down. To keep the soil from blowing away, the SCS asked farmers to **contour plow** their fields.

A contour-plowed field

CHAPTER 3

Until It Rains

Earl came home in the middle of September. After riding the rails and hitchhiking, he arrived in the kitchen covered with dirt and dust. His mother let out a cry and threw her arms around him. Pete ran to the fields to call the men, and the whole family gathered to welcome their boy home.

That night, after feasting on roast chicken, fried pork, biscuits, canned green beans, and pie, they turned on the radio. They listened to music and danced and celebrated Earl's homecoming. Earl described swimming in the Pacific Ocean. He also told of getting lost in the sprawling city of Los Angeles. He described the bright flowers blooming in December. Patty told her jokes. Pete played his song. It was a happy time for the Bucklers, a bright spot, like a new penny shining in the dust.

Laguna Beach, California

from Patty's diary

September 16, 1935

Earl's home!! He got here yesterday. He admired FDR and laughed at all my jokes. He's trying to persuade Pa and Ma to move to California until the drought breaks. Uncle Jack said he heard they don't like people from Oklahoma out there, and there's not enough work for everybody. Earl says that's true up in the San Joaquin Valley, but we wouldn't go there. He would take us to Los Angeles. That's where Hollywood is. I might see a movie star!

September 23, 1935

It started blowing while Pete and I were walking to school today, so we walked backwards. I told him to put on the dust mask Ma makes him carry. He didn't argue one bit. Just did it. That's not like Pete. I think that pneumonia's taking the spunk right out of him.

Speaking of brothers, Earl's been going out most every night with the Vernon boys. They drive to Goodwell or Guymon and get home late. Ma tried to keep him home last night, but Pa shushed her. He said Earl's pretty near a grown man and can go out if he wants. He went to California on his own, didn't he? But this morning I overheard Pa telling Earl that he better start doing some work around here.

from Patty's diary

September 25, 1935

Yesterday, Uncle Jack started cutting a field of sorghum. Pa and Earl hauled the grain to the barn. It was pretty thin, but it'll help get the animals through the winter. Then, last night it rained. Pa says we may get more growth out of it, and a second cutting. Uncle Jack says what little crop we got was because of all that contour plowing they did.

Ma seems real worried about Pete. He coughs a lot and doesn't have any get-up-and-go. He hasn't touched the guitar since the night Earl got here.

September 27, 1935

Dear Diary — My goodness, what a fight! I think the dust, and Earl's being home, and Pete's cough, and the way the grown-ups are always worrying just pushed everyone over the edge.

It was all about going to California. Earl <u>really</u> wants us to go. He says California has a lot of opportunities, more than here, and the air is clean. Ma is so worried about Pete that she's willing to go for the sake of his health. Grandma and Grandpa said they just won't go, period. It would be like giving up, and they're not quitters. Well! That got Ma's back up, and it just went on and on. No one asked my opinion (naturally). In the end, we didn't decide anything.

from Patty's diary

September 29, 1935

Dear Diary — A terrible thing has happened! Earl came home late and fell asleep and then woke up from the smell of smoke. His curtain was on fire! And then the sheet over his window caught, and now our part of the house is burned down! Thank heavens no one was hurt! Earl woke us up, and we all got out. (I grabbed you, and Pete grabbed the guitar.) Pa and Uncle Jack and Ma and everyone ran to the well. Thank goodness there was water. They somehow got the fire out before it spread to the main part of the house or the barn. We are lucky it wasn't blowing, or we wouldn't have anything left. Oh Diary, what are we going to do now?

September 30, 1935

We are real crowded in the house. Pa and Grandpa built that addition before Earl was born. It's pretty much gone now. Earl admitted he left a lantern burning. I've never seen Pa so mad.

We had a family talk at supper tonight. Everyone was real calm and serious. Pa and Earl are for leaving. Ma is, too, because of Pete. She also said it would help Grandpa to have clean air. But Grandpa and Grandma said no. Uncle Jack is for staying. I said if I have to choose, I guess I'm for going. Pete agreed with me.

The Buckler family made a difficult decision. They decided to split up. Wally and Ruth and the children would drive to California in the car. Grandma and Grandpa and Jack would stay on the farm. They told each other it was only temporary. The young ones would come back "when it rains."

Wally and Ruth packed the car to the roof. They took blankets and a table and two mattresses that weren't damaged in the fire. They tied those on the roof. They took clothes, dishes, tools, a coffeepot, and a skillet. Grandpa let Pete take his old guitar. Patty cried when

Wally said she couldn't take FDR, so Jack promised to take care of him. Grandma offered Ruth the radio, but Ruth said no. She knew Grandma would be lonely without it. So the radio stayed.

Before they left, Wally took a last walk through the fields. A little wheat had come up in September. Drifting sand had already smothered part of it. The rest only needed rain, but when rain would come, nobody could tell.

CHAPTER 4

Going Down the Road

The Bucklers set out in early October 1935. They drove south through the Texas Panhandle until they reached U.S. Route 66. Route 66 was a two-lane highway that stretched from Chicago, Illinois, to Santa Monica, California. It was a little more than 2,400 miles long and ran through eight states. It has been called many names, including the "Main Street of America" and "mother road."

In the 1930s, hundreds of thousands of poor **migrants** traveled west on Route 66. They came from all over the Plains and the South. Many came from the cotton-growing regions of Oklahoma, Arkansas, Missouri, and Texas. Others, like the Bucklers, came from the heart of the Dust Bowl. A good many others came from towns and cities. Wherever they started, though, they became known as "Okies" when they crossed the state line into California.

Car driving along Route 66

from Patty's diary

October 8, 1935

Dear Diary — We left home yesterday.
Last night we camped out near
Amarillo, Texas. Now we're in New
Mexico, driving west on Route 66.
It's just as dry around here as it was
at home, but not as flat or dusty.

A lot of other people are on the road
too. We saw a family hitchhiking. We
talked to some folks from Arkansas.
They heard there's a town up ahead,
Tucumcari, where you can get gas
and food. We'll eat what we brought
from home, though. Pa took money
out of the jar in the kitchen before
we left, but we need it for gas.

It was hard for me to get to sleep
last night. I lay awake wondering
what everyone was doing at home.
I bet they were listening to on the
radio. I wonder if FDR misses me.

October 9, 1935

We're camped near a filling station
and store outside of Albuquerque,
New Mexico. About a dozen other cars
full of people are camped here too.

October 10, 1935

We're in Arizona. Look at those
mountains! All kinds of strange
shapes and beautiful colors. The sun
is setting. It's like a picture postcard!

October 12, 1935

Dear Folks,
    We are at a filling station in the Black Mountains, about eight miles from a place called Oatman, Arizona. The car gave out and so did the money. I guess a lot of cars break down in these mountains. After I fix the car, I'll see if there are some other cars around here I can fix to earn some money. We'll be here a few days. Everyone is holding up fine. We have to get through the desert next. We'll write when we get somewhere.

                                        Love to all,
                                        Wally

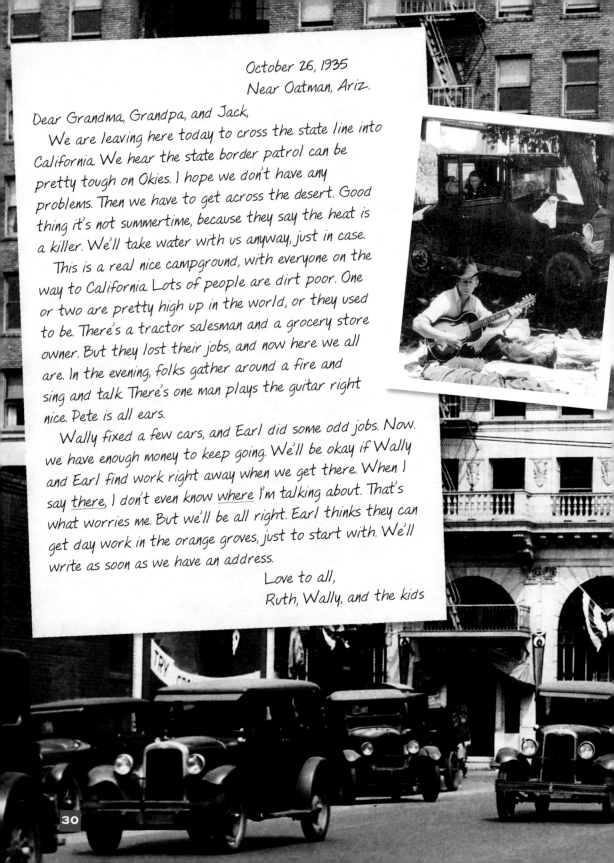

October 26, 1935
Near Oatman, Ariz.

Dear Grandma, Grandpa, and Jack,

We are leaving here today to cross the state line into California. We hear the state border patrol can be pretty tough on Okies. I hope we don't have any problems. Then we have to get across the desert. Good thing it's not summertime, because they say the heat is a killer. We'll take water with us anyway, just in case.

This is a real nice campground, with everyone on the way to California. Lots of people are dirt poor. One or two are pretty high up in the world, or they used to be. There's a tractor salesman and a grocery store owner. But they lost their jobs, and now here we all are. In the evening, folks gather around a fire and sing and talk. There's one man plays the guitar right nice. Pete is all ears.

Wally fixed a few cars, and Earl did some odd jobs. Now we have enough money to keep going. We'll be okay if Wally and Earl find work right away when we get there. When I say there, I don't even know where I'm talking about. That's what worries me. But we'll be all right. Earl thinks they can get day work in the orange groves, just to start with. We'll write as soon as we have an address.

Love to all,
Ruth, Wally, and the kids

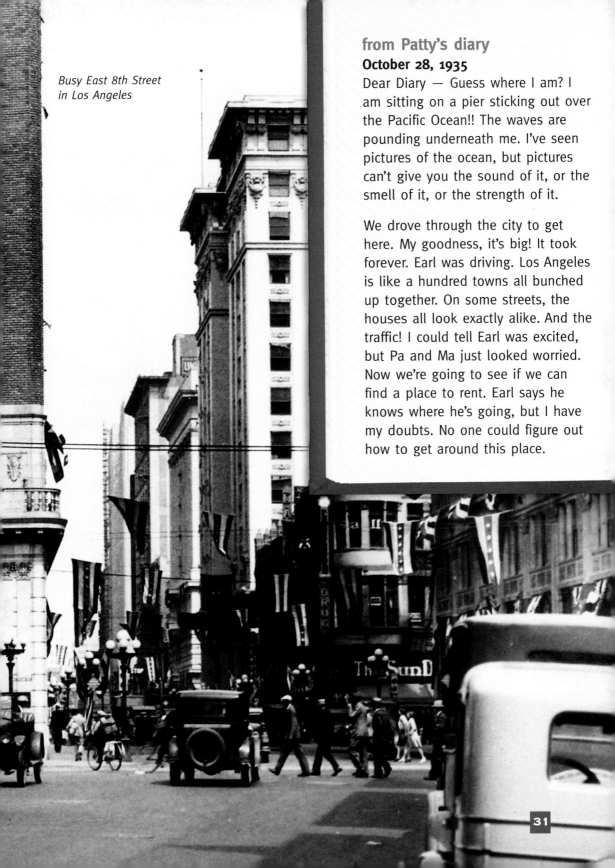

Busy East 8th Street
in Los Angeles

from Patty's diary
October 28, 1935

Dear Diary — Guess where I am? I am sitting on a pier sticking out over the Pacific Ocean!! The waves are pounding underneath me. I've seen pictures of the ocean, but pictures can't give you the sound of it, or the smell of it, or the strength of it.

We drove through the city to get here. My goodness, it's big! It took forever. Earl was driving. Los Angeles is like a hundred towns all bunched up together. On some streets, the houses all look exactly alike. And the traffic! I could tell Earl was excited, but Pa and Ma just looked worried. Now we're going to see if we can find a place to rent. Earl says he knows where he's going, but I have my doubts. No one could figure out how to get around this place.

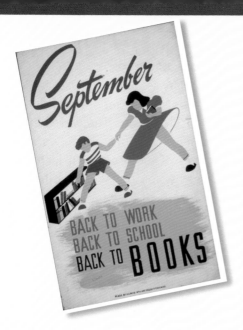

from Patty's diary

October 30, 1935

Dear Diary — We needed a place right away, and this is it. We found an auto court with cabins, and we rented one for three dollars a week. It's just one room. No kitchen and no bathroom. We are right crowded here, but Ma says we'll find a better place soon.

Earl and Pa went to the orange groves today to look for work. I hope they find jobs, I truly do. Sometimes Earl is all talk. This better not be one of those times.

November 2, 1935

Ma says we have to go to school. She wants to take us to register on Monday. I used to do real well in school back home, but I don't want to go here. I only have my two Sears dresses, and Pete has his coveralls. No one wears coveralls out here. We haven't got money for new clothes.

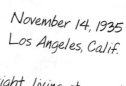

November 14, 1935
Los Angeles, Calif.

Dear Grandpa, Grandma, and Jack,

How are you all doing? Getting any rain? We are all right, living at an auto court while we look for something better.

Wally and Earl got work picking oranges. It isn't farming, but it's better than nothing. We're living on canned beans and such right now. Wally is thinking of looking around for a job as an auto mechanic. He could try to get work in a packing shed, or some other day work, but he's good with cars. Well, we'll see.

The young ones have started school. It's hard for them, being new and all. I was hoping Earl would go back and finish high school, but he says he won't.

The California air has done Pete a world of good. He's much stronger. Still crazy about that guitar. I wish he would spend half as much time doing his schoolwork as he does playing that thing. As for me, I sure am homesick. People here are not friendly, but I try not to let it bother me.

Wally and the kids send their love. We hope you're feeling better, Grandpa. Patty says to give FDR a pat from her.

Love from us all,
Ruth

The Bucklers had a rough time in the beginning. They had very little money, and city living was a big change for them. Patty and Pete were teased in school about being "Okies." Ruth was lonely.

Other migrants had it worse, though. The drought of the 1930s was forcing many cotton farmers out of Oklahoma, Arkansas, and Texas. These migrants were poor. They flocked to the San Joaquin Valley to find work picking cotton.

Most were sadly disappointed. There were not nearly enough jobs for all the migrants seeking work. Thousands of newcomers had no work and no place to live. Whole families spent winters camped by the sides of roads. The miserable living conditions left them hungry, cold, and sick.

Soon, the federal government stepped in. The Farm Security Administration built camps in the San Joaquin Valley to house the homeless migrants. The camps didn't solve every problem. The residents were still poor and out of work. Still, the camps gave them shelter and a welcome feeling of community.

CHAPTER 5

Hope on the Horizon

The Bucklers slowly settled into their new life in California. After picking oranges for a while, Wally started looking for other work. In February, he got lucky. He found a part-time job at a service station. A man who had come from Oklahoma in the 1920s owned it. Wally soon impressed his boss with his skill at fixing cars. By March, he was working full-time as an auto mechanic.

Meanwhile, back in Oklahoma, Grandpa, Grandma, and Jack were still enduring dust and drought. High winds and dust storms blew often in March and April of 1936. The dust was so thick that Jack could barely see his way between the farm buildings. People continued to move out of the area. In one week, Jack saw 11 notices in the paper announcing that family farms were being taken over by banks. The farmers couldn't repay the money they had borrowed to buy their farms. Yet there were many hopeful signs. Jack reported on them in a letter that spring.

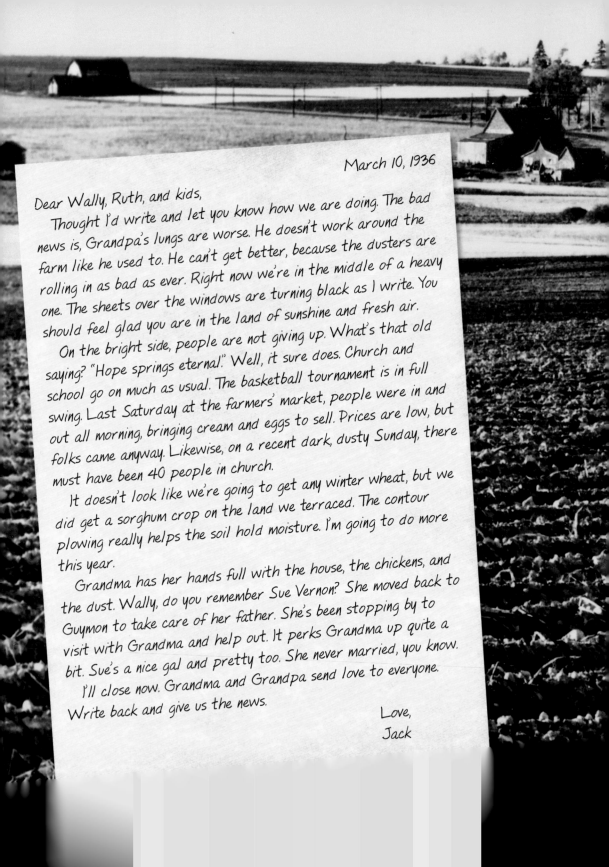

March 10, 1936

Dear Wally, Ruth, and kids,

Thought I'd write and let you know how we are doing. The bad news is, Grandpa's lungs are worse. He doesn't work around the farm like he used to. He can't get better, because the dusters are rolling in as bad as ever. Right now we're in the middle of a heavy one. The sheets over the windows are turning black as I write. You should feel glad you are in the land of sunshine and fresh air.

On the bright side, people are not giving up. What's that old saying? "Hope springs eternal." Well, it sure does. Church and school go on much as usual. The basketball tournament is in full swing. Last Saturday at the farmers' market, people were in and out all morning, bringing cream and eggs to sell. Prices are low, but folks came anyway. Likewise, on a recent dark, dusty Sunday, there must have been 40 people in church.

It doesn't look like we're going to get any winter wheat, but we did get a sorghum crop on the land we terraced. The contour plowing really helps the soil hold moisture. I'm going to do more this year.

Grandma has her hands full with the house, the chickens, and the dust. Wally, do you remember Sue Vernon? She moved back to Guymon to take care of her father. She's been stopping by to visit with Grandma and help out. It perks Grandma up quite a bit. Sue's a nice gal and pretty too. She never married, you know.

I'll close now. Grandma and Grandpa send love to everyone. Write back and give us the news.

Love,
Jack

Bell Gardens, Calif.
May 1, 1936

Dear Grandma, Grandpa, and Jack,

How are you all doing? We have a lot of news. First, we have moved. We bought a little house in a place called Bell Gardens. We found it through an advertisement. It's only $20 down and $10 each month. It's a little ways out of the city. We have a backyard and a well. The soil is good, and I'm planning a vegetable garden. I'd like to get some chickens too. Most everyone here is new, and no one has much money. I've even met folks from Oklahoma! I think the kids are happier, and I am too.

Second, after Wally got his new job, Earl took off again. He hitchhiked up to San Francisco to see what that's like. He said he's thinking about going farther north to try logging. That boy just can't stay still.

We send our love to everyone and get-well wishes to Grandpa. Maybe you could visit sometime. The fresh air would certainly do him good.

Love,

Ruth, Wally, and the kids

P.S. Patty says if you do come visit, bring FDR. We can build a rabbit hutch in the backyard for him.

from Patty's diary
June 3, 1936

Dear Diary — I can't believe school is almost over! Ma and Pa are proud of my good grades, and I am too. But it's hard. I've been trying to change the way I talk so I don't sound like an Okie. I'm proud of being from Oklahoma, but I hate being teased. In school, we Okies act real tough, like we don't care. But we do. I do.

On Saturday we drove to the next town to buy me a bathing suit. When I was trying it on, I heard two girls talking in the next changing room. One said something about "dumb Okies." The other one said "so many Okies are moving to Bell Gardens that they're changing the name to Billy Goat Acres." Ha ha, very funny.

All the Bucklers missed Oklahoma. They often thought about going back. But by the time the drought ended, they were settled in Bell Gardens. They'd made friends, and Wally had been promoted at work. They decided to stay on.

Rain began falling on the southern Great Plains in 1938. There were fewer and fewer dust storms. There were 61 big dusters in 1938. There were 30 in 1939, and 17 in 1940.

The Buckler farm in Oklahoma stayed in the family. After a long period of ill health, Grandpa died of lung disease in 1937. Grandma lived on the farm with Jack. He eventually married Sue Vernon, and they had one son. The son owns the farm today.

Earl Buckler worked as a logger and a truck driver. When the United States entered World War II, he joined the Marine Corps. He was killed on the Pacific island of Guadalcanal in 1942.

Patty Buckler became the first member of her family to graduate from college. She became an English teacher and moved back to Oklahoma, settling near Tulsa.

Pete Buckler never stopped "fooling around" on the guitar. After graduating from high school, he moved to Bakersfield, California, where he joined a country-western band. He had a long career as a musician.

Glossary

contour plow–to plow following ridges and furrows of land to reduce erosion of topsoil

drought–a long period of very little or no rainfall

Dust Bowl–the area of the Great Plains where dust storms are common

erosion–a gradual wearing away of soil by water or wind

homesteader–a person who is granted public land by the U.S. government for the purpose of settling there

migrants–people who move from one place to another in search of work or to settle

New Deal–the policies and programs intoduced by President Franklin D. Roosevelt in the 1930s to improve ecomonic and social conditions in the United States

oxygen tent–a small tent placed over the head and shoulders of someone who has trouble breathing. It is supplied with a steady flow of oxygen.